SHIN YOSHIDA

Yuya, Yuto, Yuri and Yugo... Finally they're all here,
and the mystery surrounding this quartet kicks off!
Look forward to both the mystery and the Duels!

NAOHITO MIYOSHI

What would I do if I had three additional personalities?
Yuto would handle the rough layouts, Yugo would ink
and Yuri would add the finishing touches! Heh heh heh...
Huh? Me? I'd be sleeping like a log! :-)

MASAHIRO HIKOKUBO

Sometimes, I fantasize about a project called Yu-Gi-Go!,
in which you can get cards all over town, and cafés and
game centers are Duel Fields, and you can unlock rare
packs by walking around a lot!! Um, sorry about that...

2

SHONEN JUMP MANGA EDITION

ORIGINAL CONCEPT BY
Kazuki Takahashi

PRODUCTION SUPPORT: **STUDIO DICE**

STORY BY
Shin Yoshida

ART BY
Naohito Miyoshi

DUEL COORDINATOR
Masahiro Hikokubo

TRANSLATION + ENGLISH ADAPTATION
Taylor Engel and John Werry, HC Language Solutions, Inc.

TOUCH-UP ART + LETTERING **John Hunt**

DESIGNER **Shawn Carrico**

EDITOR **Mike Montesa**

YU-GI-OH! ARC-V © 2014 by Kazuki Takahashi, Shin Yoshida, Naohito Miyoshi, Masahiro Hikokubo/SHUEISHA Inc.
Based on Animation TV series YU-GI-OH! ARC-V
© 1996 Kazuki Takahashi
© 2014 NAS • TV TOKYO

The stories, characters and incidents mentioned in this
publication are entirely fictional.

Printed in the U.S.A.

Published by VIZ Media, LLC
P.O. Box 77010
San Francisco, CA 94107

10 9 8 7 6 5 4 3 2 1
First printing, September 2017

www.viz.com

www.shonenjump.com

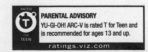

2

Turbo Duel!!

ORIGINAL CONCEPT BY **Kazuki Takahashi**

PRODUCTION SUPPORT: **STUDIO DICE**

STORY BY **Shin Yoshida**

ART BY **Naohito Miyoshi**

DUEL COORDINATOR **Masahiro Hikokubo**

CHARACTERS

Yuya Sakaki

A Dueltainer who entertains everybody. He's searching for the Genesis Omega Dragon.

Yuto

Another personality inside Yuya. He uses XYZ Summons.

?

?

Shuzo Hiragi

The principal of Syu Zo Duel School, which is currently experiencing financial difficulties.

Yuzu Hiragi

She scouted Yuya for her father Shuzo's cram school.

Reiji Akaba

President of the Leo Corporation. He's using his company to hunt Yuya.

Shun Kurosaki

The Leo Corporation's second assassin. He challenged Yuya to a no-holds-barred Duel!

Sora Shiunin

Although he wants to duel Yuya, he is concerned about Akaba's enigmatic behavior.

Shingo Sawatari

The first Leo Corporation Duelist to face off against Yuya.

STORY

Solid Vision with mass has plunged the world into the era of Action Duels. The Duelists of the Leo Corporation are in hot pursuit of Yuya Sakaki, a Dueltainer who can hack that technology. The Leo Corporation's first assassin, Sawatari, squares off against him only to discover that the person he has been chasing is someone else—a guy who introduces himself as Yuto! However, during the Duel, Yuto transforms into Yuya, who wins and escapes. Yuzu Hiragi, who happens to be present at the Duel, becomes Yuya's manager and joins him in pursuit of the Genesis Omega Dragon [G.O.D.]. Then the second assassin, Kurosaki, takes Yuzu's father, Shuzo, hostage and Yuya ends up dueling him. After winning, Yuya tells Yuzu and her father that he has four personalities!!

2 Turbo Duel!!

YUGO...

...WON'T THEY GET SUSPICIOUS IF WE DON'T GO BACK SOON?

Yu-Gi-Oh! ARC-V
Scale 7: Genesis Omega Dragon!!

DON'T WORRY!

I ASKED YUTO TO COVER FOR US.

Yu-Gi-Oh! ARC-V
Scale 7: Genesis Omega Dragon!!

I DON'T.

IF I DID, I WOULDN'T BE ERASING HIS MEMORIES.

...YOU WANT YUYA TO REMEMBER YOU.

DON'T TELL ME...

BA

MF

YUYA DOESN'T NEED TO REMEMBER US.

I HOPE THAT'S TRUE.

IT WOULD ONLY MAKE HIM SAD.

I KNOW.

A QUADRUPLE PERSONALITY...?!

I HAVEN'T SEEN THE OTHER TWO LATELY. WHERE DID THEY GO?

A LOT HAS HAPPENED TO ME...

...AND MY MEMORY IS FULL OF HOLES!

I DON'T KNOW WHY, BUT I HAVE THREE OTHER PERSONALITIES INSIDE.

G.O.D.!
(GENESIS
OMEGA
DRAGON)

ARE YOUR MISSING MEMORIES AND QUADRUPLE PERSONALITY RELATED TO THAT *GENESIS OMEGA DRAGON* YOU MENTIONED?

HEY, YUYA?

THAT'S MORE THAN A LITTLE...

... WHOEVER HAS THAT CARD CAN DESTROY THE WORLD.

YOU MIGHT NOT BELIEVE THIS, BUT...

IT'S A CARD THAT WILL DECIDE THE FATE OF THE WORLD.

WHAT DO YOU MEAN?

DESTROY THE WORLD?!

IT'S POSSIBLE THAT THE SOLID VISION SYSTEM WAS MADE SPECIFICALLY TO CREATE IT.

GENESIS OMEGA DRAGON IS THE ULTIMATE MONSTER. IT ABUSES THE SYSTEM THAT MAKES SOLID VISION PHYSICALLY REAL.

BUT HOW DO YOU KNOW THAT, YUYA?!

NOPE... I CAN'T KEEP UP...

NEVER MIND! JUST FIX THAT CATCHPHRASE!

IT'S TOO EMBARRASSING! I REFUSE TO SAY IT!

I SAW IT IN A DREAM.

HUH?!

I'M NOT DUELING FOR YOUR PUBLICITY!

I'M GOING BACK TO MY HIDEOUT!

WHAT?!

BUT WE GOTTA ADVERTISE SYU 20 DUEL SCHOOL!

Y-YOU ARE?

STUMBLE

AND I'M GOING WITH YOU!!

BUT...

...I'VE COME PREPARED!

TA-DA! GLOVES WITH PRESIDENT AKABA'S FINGERPRINTS!!

AND GLASSES WITH HIS RETINAL PATTERN!!

HEH! ♡

GOOD THING I MADE THESE IN SECRET!

LEO CORPORATION
- LOCKED -

HUH ?!

YOU CAN'T GET IN HERE WITH THOSE.

I WEAR SPECIAL CONTACTS TO PREVENT THEFT OF MY RETINAL PATTERN.

SO I GUESS...

...I GOT IN BECAUSE...

INSTEAD OF DOING THIS, YOU SHOULD BE FOCUSED ON YOUR WORK.

URGH...

BECAUSE I *LET* YOU IN.

SLUMP

WELL, YOU SEE...

UNLIKE THOSE SIMPLETONS, I CAN'T CONCENTRATE WHEN I HAVE QUESTIONS.

THEN ALLOW *ME* TO ANSWER IN PLACE OF THE COMPUTER.

YEAH, THAT'S EASIER!

AND WHAT'S A PENDULUM SUMMONS? AND ARE YOU REALLY AFTER HIM BECAUSE HE'S A HACKER?

WHO IS YUYA SAKAKI?

HE SAYS HE'S A MAGICIAN, BUT CARDS THAT PRODUCE PHYSICAL SOLID VISION MUST BE SOME KIND OF TECHNOLOGY!

...BUT YOU MAY NOT BELIEVE ME.

FINE, I'LL TELL YOU....

...WHO WILL SOMEDAY DESTROY THIS WORLD.

HE IS THE *DESTINY FACTOR*...

...THE WORLD?

DESTROY...

BUT HE WILL SOON WALK THAT PATH.

HOW DO YOU KNOW THE FUTURE?

HE'S PLOTTING A THING LIKE *THAT*?!

HE SURE DIDN'T LOOK LIKE IT, BUT...

IT DID?

THE MOTHER COMPUTER PREDICTED IT.

ANYWAY, I ALSO WANTED TO ASK...

...ABOUT *YOU*, PRESIDENT AKABA.

IS THAT REALLY TRUE?

I FEEL SO GROWN-UP! I'VE ALWAYS WANTED TO WEAR A SUIT!

DO I LOOK SMART?

YOU LOOK GOOD, YUTO! LIKE A SHARP BUSINESS-MAN!

QUIT FOOLING AROUND!

LOOKS LIKE MY COMPLIMENT FED HIS EGO...

HEH...

I CAN'T BELIEVE IT!

WE GOT IN!

BIP BIP

BIP

I.D. card

YUYA'S A GENIUS AT MAKING THINGS LIKE THIS.

DING

WE'LL GO THERE FIRST...

...AND HOPEFULLY FIND SOME CLUES.

GENESIS OMEGA DRAGON'S DATA CAME FROM THE SYSTEM LABORATORY.

BIP

AND? WHERE ARE WE GOING?

WAS THIS A *TRAP*?

HUH ?!

IT WON'T OPEN!

DO

THE DOOR...

OM

I'VE BEEN WAITING FOR YOU, YUYA SAKAKI.

THAT'S RIGHT.

FIN SH

FNA H

!

SHUN KUROSAKI

SHUN KUROSAKI

DRAFT 1 CHARACTER

KUROSAKI
AGE 17
A COOL, HANDSOME GUY.
LOOKS SMART.

THE TALLEST
OF THE THREE.
MAYBE
DIFFERENTIATE HIS
UNIFORM FROM THE
OTHER TWO.

In the early designs, Kurosaki was slimmer than he is now, and he was more of the cool, handsome type. The idea that he's always hungry for a fight came up later.

WELL, IT'S KINDA HARD TO TALK ABOUT MYSELF.

ALL RIGHT, THEN— LET'S DUEL.

THERE ARE QUESTIONS I WANT TO ASK YOU.

SO... UH... ABOUT THE GENESIS OMEGA DRAGON...

LIKE WHERE YOU COME FROM.

ARGH

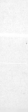

SO, HE DOESN'T KNOW...

NOT A CLUE.

SORA HAS SUCCEEDED IN LURING OUT YUYA SAKAKI.

WHOSE SIDE ARE YOU ON?!

SORA WILL NEVER BEAT YUYA SAKAKI!

HE'S TRAPPED LIKE A RAT! WE SHOULD GO TOO!

YOU? RIDICULOUS!

WHAT?!

THAT'S MY LINE!

I'M THE ONLY ONE WHO CAN DEFEAT HIM.

NO.

AH, FORGET IT!

ANYWAY, WE'RE GOING THERE.

IF WE STAY HERE, WE CAN WATCH SOMETHING INTERESTING.

HE'S ALREADY SURROUNDED.

LOOK AT ALL THE CUTE SWEETS!

WHOA!

I'M GOING TO SHOW YOU SOME TRUE HOSPI-TALITY!

THIS SHOULD BE FUN...

HOO

IT EXPLODED?!!

YUYA!!

BOOOOM

HEH HEH HEH! BE CAREFUL.

SOME OF THE TRAPS ARE WORSE THAN OTHERS!

NOW THAT'S TWO FOR ME! ♡

WOOO

SO IT SEEMS...

ENTER-MATE BARRACUDA

ATK 500 DEF 1100

ENTER-MATE BALLAD

ATK 500 DEF 1100

PS 5

WHY
DIDN'T
YOU USE
THEM
SOONER
?!

YUYA!

PS 2

WHAT A
COUPLE OF
HOTTIES!

OH,
WOW!

GO, HANDSOME LIGER! ATTACK FRIGHTFUR BEAR!!

ONCE PER TURN, WHEN AN ENTER-MATE MONSTER ATTACKS, IT DROPS THE ENEMY MONSTER'S ATK BY 600!

I ACTIVATE ENTER-MATE BALLAD'S PENDULUM EFFECT!

ENTER-MATE BALLAD

When an Enter-Mate Monster attacks, reduce the ATK of your opponent's monster by 600.

ATK 500 DEF 1100

AT THE SAME TIME, I ACTIVATE ENTER-MATE BARRACUDA'S PENDULUM EFFECT!

ENTER-MATE BARRACUDA

When the values of a card on your opponent's field change, double the values of that change.

ATK 500 DEF 1100

URGH ...

ATK 1600

YUYA, ACTIVATE A TRAP! YOU'VE GOT **ENTER-MATE SHOW UP** FACE DOWN ON YOUR FIELD. IT DOUBLES ONE ENTER-MATE MONSTER'S ATK!

I KNOW! I ACTIVATE THE TRAP CARD...

FWIP

FWIP

HAH!

I...

!

WHO'S THE GIRL?

YOUR KID SISTER?

SINCE THIS MONSTER WAS DESTROYED IN BATTLE, I CAN USE THIS AS AN EQUIP CARD, BOOSTING ATK BY 1,000!

FRIGHTFUR BEAR

Equip a Monster destroyed in battle as an Equip Card that boosts ATK by 1000 points.

ATK 2200 DEF 1800

ATK 3200

OH NO... THAT POOR HOTTIE...

FORGIVE ME, YUYA!

I SET ONE CARD FACE DOWN AND END MY TURN!

IT'S ALL REIJI AKABA'S FAULT!

TAKING HOSTAGES IS INEXCUSABLE.

IT'S IN-HUMAN!

DEPENDING ON YOUR ANSWER, I MAY DISPENSE JUSTICE!

ANSWER ME, REIJI AKABA!

...

BUT HE ALSO TOOK A HOSTAGE HIMSELF...

THAT VOICE...

HEY NOW...

THIS LOOKS LIKE A JOB FOR ME!

SHWOOOSH

WAGH!

HMPH!

YOU'RE MUCH TOO SOFT...

!

...YUYA.

SORA SHIUNIN

DRAFT I CHARACTER
SORA SHIUNIN
Age 13

His childish appearance makes him seem likely to act spoiled.

Sora's hairstyle and atmosphere haven't changed much since his early designs. About the only difference is that his clothes are more casual now. That drawing of him with glasses is rare!

GWOOOO

THIS KID REEKS LIKE VULGAR SCUM!

Yu-Gi-Oh! ARC-V
Scale 9: Fusion vs. Fusion!!

DID HE TURN INTO SOMEONE ELSE?

HIS PER-SONALITY IS WAY DIFFER-ENT!

WHAT...

...IS WITH THIS GUY?

ALL RIGHT, YOU'RE DUELING ME NOW!

MY TURN! I DRAW!

FWIPP

Yu-Gi-Oh! ARC-V
Scale 9: Fusion vs. Fusion!!

IS THIS YUYA'S *THIRD* PERSONALITY?

I ACTIVATE A SPELL CARD!

PEN-DULLUM FUSION!

PENDULUM FUSION (SPELL CARD)

Use Pendulum Zone cards to Fusion Summon.

THIS CARD LETS ME USE PENDULLUM ZONE CARDS IN FUSION SUMMONS!

URGH!

FROM THE PENDULUM ZONE, I FUSE ENTER-MATE BALLAD AND ENTER-MATE BARRACUDA!!

HE USES FUSION TOO?!

FU-SION...

ENTER-MATE BARRACUDA

ATK 500 DEF 1100

ENTER-MATE BALLAD

ATK 500 DEF 1100

COME FORTH, PREDATOR PLANT *CHIMERA RAFFLESIA*!!

FUSION SUMMONS!!

AND IF YOU FUSE TWO HOTTIES...

YA

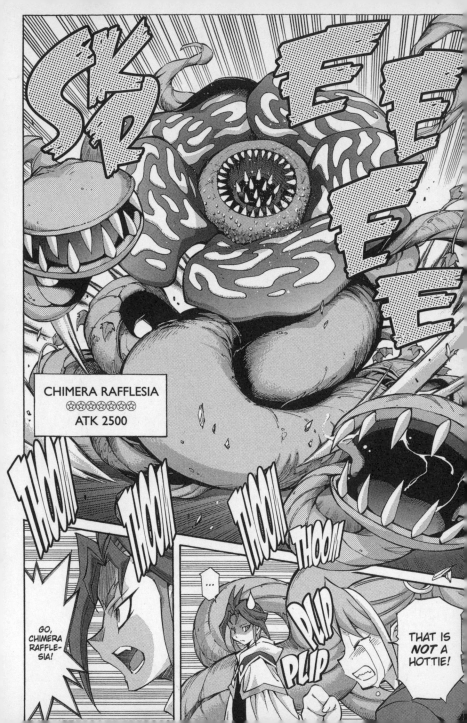

FWOOOOOSH

FRIGHTFUR BEAR
ATK 3200

WHEN THIS CARD DOES BATTLE, THE ATK OF MY OPPONENT'S MONSTER RETURNS TO ITS ORIGINAL VALUE AND MY CARD'S ATK IS BOOSTED BY THE AMOUNT IT LOSES!

I ACTIVATE CHIMERA RAFFLESIA'S EFFECT!

DON'T WORRY, KID! I'M NOT THAT GENEROUS!

OH, I GET IT!

BUT WITH THAT ATK, YOU CAN'T...

YOU'RE GONNA *HELP* ME!

THOOM THOOM THOOM THOOM THOOM THOOM

ATK 2500

AFTER BATTLE, CHIMERA RAFFLESIA'S ATK RETURNS TO NORMAL!

WHEN HIS APPEARANCE CHANGED, SO DID HIS DUELING STYLE!

LP 1900

INNER VOICE? YOU STOLE MY BODY!

I PREFER MY INNER VOICES TO REMAIN *SILENT.*

HEY, YURI! THAT'S TOO MUCH!

HE'S GOT—

THAT KID IS A *LIAR.*

I SAID DON'T WORRY.

DON'T YOU GET IT?

WHAT DO YOU MEAN?

EVERYONE HIDES DARKNESS INSIDE...

...DARKNESS THEY REFUSE TO REVEAL...

HE IS?!

!

KEH HEH HEH...

AH HA HA!

A GUY WHO BLABS IT ALL OVER...

...IS JUST VULGAR SCUM!

YOU'RE A *BAD BOY!* SO I'M GONNA *SCHOOL* YOU!!

BA

RRIP★

YOU'RE RIGHT!

I WAS LYING ABOUT EVERYTHING!

M

FINE, I'LL OWN UP TO IT...

WHAT'S GOING ON?!

HUH?! BUT THAT PHOTO...

CRUMMBLE

DA

FMP

IT WAS...

...ALL A LIE ?!

N...

NO, THAT WASN'T...

...I SHALL KEEP THAT IN MIND.

DON'T WORRY ABOUT IT.

IF THAT MADE ME LOOK LIKE SCUM TO YOU...

FWOO°

KNOCK IT OFF!!

KEH... KEH HEH HEH!

TRMBL

TRMBL

MY TURN!

I DRAW!

WELL, THAT'S OKAY.

FWOO O O

I THOUGHT THE PHANTOM WAS A PUSHOVER...

...BUT I GUESS I WAS WRONG.

I ACTIVATE THE VERY ACTION CARD YOU'RE TARGETING!

REACTION DRAW (SPELL CARD)

When this card is destroyed, draw one card from your deck.

GUESS I'M THE ONE WITH THE ACTION CARD ADVANTAGE!

I DRAW!

RE- ACTION DRAW!

FLUFFAL FUSIONIST

YOUR TRUMP CARD?!

IN OTHER WORDS, MY *REAL* ENTERTAIN- MENT!

AND EVERY- THING IS IN PLACE...

...SO IT'S TIME FOR MY TRUMP CARD!

...DEVELOPED THAT CARD AS A PROTOTYPE.

THE LEO CORPORATION...

WHY DID HE USE A PENDULUM SUMMONS?!

NOW WE CAN COLLECT MORE DATA THAN EVER ON YUYA SAKAKI!

BABMP

BAMM!!

RMMMM

BUT... WHAT'S WITH THAT IMPACT?

!

YUYA!

RMMMM

YURI, ARE YOU OKAY?!

LP 1600

AND NOW ...

THIS IS MY STYLE OF ENTERTAINMENT DUEL!!

...I ACTIVATE FRIGHTFUR DAREDEVIL'S EFFECT!!

SHING

UGH!

THOOM

LP 1100

WHEN THIS HAS DESTROYED A MONSTER, IT DOES 1,000 DAMAGE TO MY OPPONENT!

GRUNG

GAGH!

LP 100

AKABA!

WHY DIDN'T YOU GIVE THAT CARD TO *ME*?!

HE'S STRONG...

SUCH INCREDIBLE STRENGTH!

Y U Y A !

SWMP

THE CARD WE DEVELOPED JUST HAPPENED TO BE MOST COMPATIBLE WITH HIM.

I WASN'T SHOWING FAVORITISM.

...SO I TRIPLED SOLID VISION'S DAMAGE SETTINGS.

HEH HEH... THIS IS A DUEL LABORATORY...

THAT ONE RATTLED MY BRAIN...

ARE YOU OKAY, YURI?!

YOU REALLY *ARE* SCUM!

RMMMMM

BUT THAT'S DANGEROUS!!

HE'S DOING SERIOUS DAMAGE!

IT'S MY FAULT WE LOST SO MUCH LIFE, BUT...

BUT HE'S RIGHT. EVEN IF WE SWITCH, YOU MIGHT COLLAPSE.

BUT I'M WORRIED.

THEN PERHAPS THERE'S HOPE FOR ME YET...

WHAT?! BUT YOU REVEALED HIS LIES!

BESIDES, THERE'S SOMETHING I WANNA TELL HIM!

NO...I THINK SHE'LL SURVIVE!

SHE LIKES HOTTIES. WILL IT DISAPPOINT HER IF I DISAPPEAR?

YURI

Purple Yuya

Here's Yuri, who entered the story as Yuya's third personality. His design hasn't changed much since early on. Was his ability to spot "vulgar scum" there from the beginning too?

Yu-Gi-Oh! ARC-V
Scale 10:
The Entertainment Ends!!

...

WHAT'S HE THINKING?!

THAT'S CRAZY... THAT WOULD INCREASE HIS OWN DAMAGE!

IN OTHER WORDS, THAT ATTACK DROPPED MY LIFE TO ZERO.

...AND I ONLY HAD 1,900 LIFE POINTS LEFT.

IT'S 2,400 ATK AGAINST 500...

THIS IS OUR CHANCE.

RETRIEVE SORA.

AND I WANT TO SEARCH YUYA SAKAKI'S MEMORIES.

...EVE. AS YOU WISH...

SORA...

YUYA...

SPSHH

WHAT THE?!

HM?

IS THAT GIRL...?

RIGHT NOW, I'M WORRIED ABOUT YUYA. THE DAMAGE SEEMS BAD.

BUT HOW CAN THIS BE?

YUYA'S MEMORIES ARE CONFUSED, SO HE HASN'T NOTICED.

UGH

DON'T EVEN. YOUR SYMPATHY WILL MAKE ME SUPER DEPRESSED!

HUH?!

I'M SORRY. I WAS RIGHT THERE, BUT...

IT WASN'T YOUR FAULT, YURI. THE ENEMY WAS TOUGH.

THAT'S ENOUGH, YOU TWO!

AND YOU WERE THE ONE WHO—

WHAT?! I COVERED FOR YOU!

!

HUH?!

HEY, YOU'RE NOT OUR BOSS!

KRAKL

KRAKL

HANG ON A MINUTE.

SOMETHING BAD IS HAPPENING.

SOMEONE'S HACKING US!

ZZZT

ZZZT

WHAT ?!

KIRI

KRAK!

HE'S WEARING IT. WE HAVE TO GET IT OFF HIM!

INTRUDERS?! WHERE'S YUYA'S DUEL DISK?!

YUGO

White Yuya

Yugo duels on a Duel Runner, so he wears riding gear in the main story, but he doesn't in these sketches. He also looks more laid-back.

WILL HE BE ALL RIGHT?

HE GETS WORKED UP EASILY.

YUGO RUSHED OFF...

HE'LL CATCH UP TO THE INTRUDER QUICKLY.

I'M CONCERNED, BUT HE'S EXCELLENT WITH A DUEL RUNNER.

WOO

HANG IN THERE, YUYA...

...

WHITE CIRCLE REEF
(SPELL CARD)

Destroy one White Monster on your field and add one monster with the same name from your deck to your hand.

I ALSO ACTIVATE A SPELL CARD! WHITE CIRCLE REEF!

A MONSTER THAT MAKES DIRECT ATTACKS?!

IS HE GONNA USE THAT TO WHITTLE DOWN MY LIFE POINTS?

BOOM

THIS CARD LETS ME DESTROY ONE OF MY OWN WHITE MONSTERS AND ADD ONE WITH THE SAME NAME FROM MY DECK TO MY HAND!

BAM

WHITE MIRROR
(SPELL CARD)

Special Summon one White Monster from the Graveyard and add one monster with the same name from your deck to your hand.

I ACTIVATE ANOTHER SPELL CARD! WHITE MIRROR!

THE SAME MONSTER? AND HE DIDN'T DO A DIRECT ATTACK?

WHAT'S HE PLANNING?!

I SPECIAL SUMMON ONE WHITE MONSTER FROM THE GRAVEYARD AND ADD A MONSTER BEARING THE SAME NAME FROM MY DECK TO MY HAND!

I SPECIAL SUMMON *WHITE MORAY*!!

WHITE PROSPERITY (SPELL CARD)

From your hand, Special Summon two White Monsters that are LV 4 or lower and have the same name.

...AND ACTIVATE A NEW SPELL CARD! *WHITE PROSPERITY*!!

I ADD ONE MORE WHITE MORAY TO MY HAND...

THIS CARD SPECIAL SUMMONS FROM MY HAND TWO WHITE MONSTERS WITH THE SAME NAME THAT ARE LEVEL 4 OR LOWER!!

I CAN'T SHAKE HIM! HE'S TOO FAST!

YOUR FRUSTRATION OVER LOSING YOUR LEAD IS OBVIOUS.

AND THE HARDER I PRESS YOU...

...THE MORE MISTAKES YOU'LL MAKE!!

NOW IT'S MY TURN!

YOU'RE NOT GETTING PAST ME!!

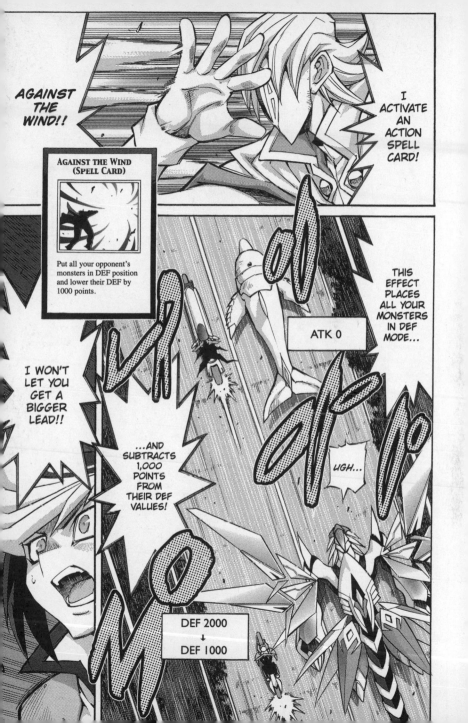

REN

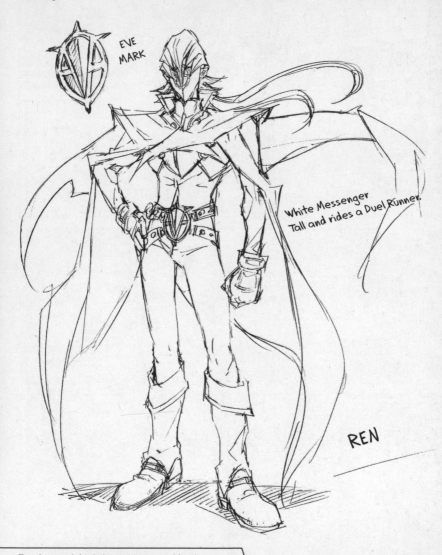

EVE MARK

White Messenger
Tall and rides a Duel Runner.

REN

Ren is an original character created for the manga.
There's probably a lot more to him than we've seen
so far. Will the "Eve" character who's been appearing
from time to time turn out to be a big part of the story?

WOOO

YUGO
...

YUGO
...

Yu-Gi-Oh! ARC-V
Scale 12:
High-Speed Strategy!!

WHAT'S
GOING
ON?!

YUYA,
WHAT'S
WRONG
?

GET
YOURSELF
TOGETHER!

A ROAD RISING FROM THE VALLEY FLOOR?

BA A AM M

YUYA SAKAKI ...

DID HIS CONSCIOUSNESS SENSE THE DANGER TO YUGO?

SKRCEEEE

WOBBLE

WOBBLE

THRUM

THRUM

THRUM

I HATE TO ADMIT IT, BUT THIS GUY'S GOT SKILLS.

I CAN BARELY EVEN STAY IN HIS SLIPSTREAM.

HE HANDLES THE COURSE EFFICIENTLY, TURNS HIS DUEL RUNNER ON A DIME...

...AND BASICALLY RIDES PERFECTLY.

I'LL GIVE UP ON TAKING THE LEAD TO GET ACTION CARDS AND JUST FOCUS ON FINDING A WAY TO BREAK THROUGH...

I DRAW!

MY TURN!

AT THE END OF THIS TURN, FOLLOW WING'S EFFECT ENDS AND CLEARWING'S ATK RETURNS TO NORMAL!

FM

THE FOURTH ACTION CARD!!

VWUM

ATK 3000
↓
ATK 2500

00

ONCE PER TURN, IT CAN HALVE AN ENEMY MONSTER'S ATK!

VR

00

VWM
W

I ACTIVATE WHITE AURA DOLPHIN'S EFFECT!!

WHAT
?!

I TUNE
WHITE
MORAY,
LEVEL 2,
WITH
WHITE
AURA
DOLPHIN,
LEVEL 6!!

HEH!

AND
CLEARWING'S
EFFECT IS
JUST WHAT
I WAS
WAITING
FOR!

WHITE SALVATION
(SPELL CARD)

Once per turn, add one
White Monster from
the Graveyard to your
hand.

FROM MY
HAND, I
ACTIVATE A
CONTINUOUS
SPELL CARD!
WHITE
SALVATION!

ATK 600

GREAT
WHALE
SLUMBER-
ING
IN
THE
ABYSS,
AWAKEN
IN THE
DEEP
BETWEEN
LIFE AND
DEATH!

I
SUMMON
WHITE
MORAY!!

ONCE PER
TURN, I
TAKE ONE
WHITE
MONSTER
FROM THE
GRAVEYARD
AND ADD IT
TO MY HAND!

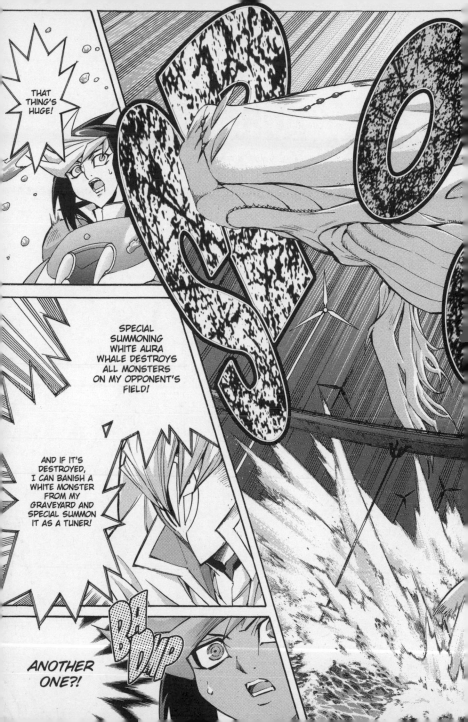

I FIGHT BACK WITH AN ACTION SPELL! *PROTECTIVE WIND!!*

PROTECTIVE WIND
(SPELL CARD)

Negate destruction from monster effects.

IT NEGATES DESTRUCTION DUE TO MONSTER EFFECTS!!

AGAINST THE WIND
(SPELL CARD)

Put all your opponent's monsters in DEF position and lower their DEF by 1000 points.

THIS EFFECT PUTS ALL YOUR MONSTERS IN DEFENSE MODE AND DROPS THEIR DEF VALUES BY 1,000!!

AH, BUT I TOO ACTIVATE AN ACTION SPELL! *AGAINST THE WIND!*

WHITE MORAY

WHITE SALVATION (SPELL CARD)

Summoned normally, this can directly attack your opponent. When Special Summoned from the Graveyard, it becomes a Tuner Monster.

ATK 600 DEF 200

Once per turn, add one White Monster from the Graveyard to your hand.

HE THINKS HE HAS SHUT DOWN MY SYNCHRO, BUT WHITE MORAY IN MY GRAVEYARD HAS AN ATK OF 600 AND CAN ATTACK DIRECTLY.

IF I USE WHITE SALVATION TO SUMMON IT NORMALLY ON MY NEXT TURN, THE DUEL WILL BE OVER.

...

ON THIS TURN, SYNCHRO PANIC'S EFFECT SAVES PASSING RIDER FROM DESTRUCTION!

THRUM

SCREE

YUGO
LP 300

I ACTIVATE A CONTINUOUS TRAP!! SYNCHRO ZONE!!

SYNCHRO ZONE (TRAP CARD)

Negate all attacks from non-Synchro monsters.

SO JUST TO BE SAFE...

DOES HE HAVE ANOTHER TRICK UP HIS SLEEVE?

HOWEVER, I'M SURE HE KNOWS THAT...

THIS CARD NEGATES ALL ATTACKS EXCEPT ONES FROM SYNCHRO MONSTERS! I JUST STOPPED YOUR ATTACKS COLD!!

BH

?!

YOUR REINCARNATION SYNCHRO'S BIGGEST FEATURE IS TURNING MONSTERS RESURRECTED FROM THE GRAVEYARD INTO TUNERS.

BUT YOU DON'T HAVE A PATENT ON CHANGING MONSTER TRAITS!!

FROM MY HAND, I ACTIVATE THE SPELL CARD *PENDULUM TRANSFER!*

I CAN DO THIS!

I'VE GOT A CARD I EVOLVED WITH YUYA!!

VROOOM

FWIP

ITS EFFECT MOVES MONSTERS FROM MY FIELD TO MY PENDULUM ZONE!

PENDULUM TRANSFER (SPELL CARD)

Place monsters on your field in your Pendulum Zone.

FROM THE FIELD TO YOUR PENDULUM ZONE...

NO! IT CAN'T BE!!

IF YUYA HADN'T SAVED ME, RIGHT NOW I'D BE...

THEN YOU SHOULD THANK HIM.

URGH...

BADMP

BADMP

WHAT A TOUGH OPPONENT.

HE GOT AWAY?

BADMP

YEAH. BUT THIS PULSE THAT HE MENTIONED...

THE ADAM FACTOR?

HE CALLED IT THE ADAM FACTOR.

BADMP

!

An excavation site on the outskirts of Maiami City...

TAK
TAK
TAK

An underground passage

GA

WOOO

DID YOU REACH A STOPPING POINT IN YOUR RESEARCH?

HAS SOMETHING HAPPENED?

REIJI...

...DO YOU THINK THE BLOOD OF THE GODS IS *RED*?

DUEL MONSTERS?

I'M COOPERATING WITH AN OLD FRIEND TO FUSE DUEL MONSTERS AND SOLID VISION.

...

IT'S A CHALLENGE TO THE *GODS*, REIJI!

IT'S MOST INTRIGUING. DUEL MONSTERS MAY OPEN THE DOOR TO THE *DIVINE REALM*.

YU-GI-OH! ARC-V-VOL. 2-THE END

Staff
Junya Uchino
Kazuo Ochiai
Toshiaki Kato

Editing
Takahiko Aikawa

Coloring
Toru Shimizu

Support
Gallop
Wedge Holdings

STOP!

YOU'RE READING THE WRONG WAY!

Yu-Gi-Oh! ARC-V

reads from right to left, starting in the upper-right corner. Japanese is read from right to left, meaning that action, sound effects and word-balloon order are completely reversed from English order.